I SPY
With My Little Eye
LOVEY THINGS
BOOK FOR KiDS

Copyright © 2021 by Happy kids Moon

I SPY with my little eye, something beginning with...

It's an
Arrow

I SPY with my little eye, something beginning with...

It's a
Balloon

I SPY with my little eye, something beginning with...

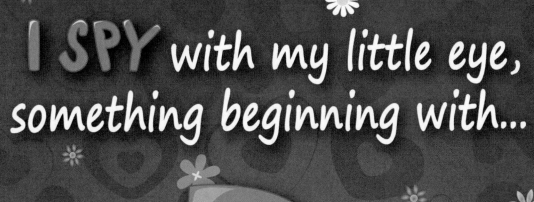

I SPY with my little eye, something beginning with...

It's a
Dove

I SPY with my little eye, something beginning with...

It's an Egg

I SPY with my little eye, something beginning with...

It's a
Flower

I SPY with my little eye, something beginning with...

It's a
Heart

It's an
Ice cream

It's a
Kite

I SPY with my little eye, something beginning with...

M

I SPY with my little eye, something beginning with...

I SPY with my little eye, something beginning with...

It's an
Octopus

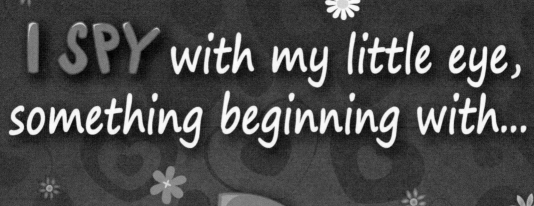

I SPY with my little eye, something beginning with...

It's a
Pizza

I SPY with my little eye, something beginning with...

It's a
Strawberry

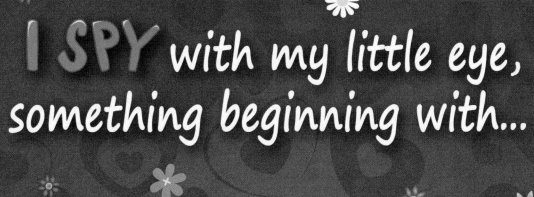

I SPY with my little eye,
something beginning with...

It's a
Teddy Bear

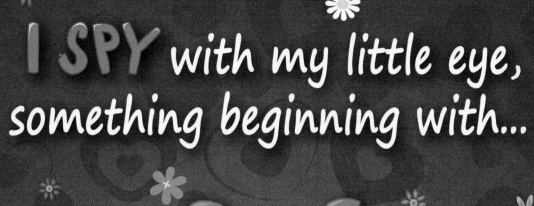

It's a Van

LOVE

It's a
Xylophone

I SPY with my little eye, something beginning with...

It's a
Yacht

Made in the USA
Las Vegas, NV
07 February 2021

17438656R00033